Lives and Times

Eli Whitney

M. C. Hall

Heinemann Library
Chicago, Illinois

Page layout by Cherylyn Bredemann
Map by John Fleck
Photo research by Amla Sanghvi

Printed and bound in the United States of America, North Mankato, MN

13 12 11
10 9 8 7 6 5 4 3 2

**Library of Congress
Cataloging-in-Publication Data**
Eli Whitney / M. C. Hall.
ISBN 1-4034-5325-X (HC), 978-1-4034-5333-4 (Pbk.)
The Cataloging-in-Publication Data for this title is on file with the Library of Congress.

062011
006213RP

Acknowledgments
The author and publishers are grateful to the following for permission to reproduce copyright material: Title page, p. 15 Bettmann/Corbis; icon (cotton), pp. 14, 28 National Cotton Council of America; icon (T-shirt) Heinemann Library; p. 4 Michael Pole/Corbis; pp. 5, 9 North Wind Picture Archives; pp. 6, 7, 10, 16, 19, 20, 23 Culver Pictures, Inc.; pp. 8, 25, 29 Library of Congress; p. 11 Kevin R. Morris/Corbis; p. 13 Telfair Museum of Art, Savannah, GA; p. 17 Kevin Fleming/Corbis; p. 18 Pond Spring, The General Joe Wheeler Home, A Property of the Alabama Historical Commission; p. 21 Manuscript and Archives/Yale University Library; pp. 22, 24, 26 New Haven Colony Historical Society; p. 27 Mark L. Stephenson/Corbis

Cover photographs by (top) National Cotton Council of America, (bottom left) New Haven Colony Historical Society, (bottom right) Bettmann/Corbis

The publisher would like to thank Charly Rimsa for her comments in the preparation of this book.

Every effort has been made to contact copyright holders of any material reproduced in this book. Any omissions will be rectified in subsequent printings if notice is given to the publisher.

Some words are shown in bold, **like this.** You can find out what they mean by looking in the glossary.

Contents

How Things Are Made

This woodworker is making a piece of furniture with simple tools.

Long ago, things like chairs and wagons were made one at a time, by hand. This took a long time. The finished things usually did not look exactly the same.

Eli Whitney found a way to make things more quickly. Different machines made different parts. Each part came out the same. Then, the parts were put together. Today, most **factories** make things this way.

This picture shows Eli in 1822.

The Early Years

This is the house where Eli was born.

Eli Whitney was born in Westborough, Massachusetts, on December 8, 1765. His parents were farmers. Eli was the first child in his family. He had one sister and two brothers.

At school Eli had trouble learning to read. But he was good at math and science. Eli also liked fixing things.

Eli liked to help his father fix tools like these.

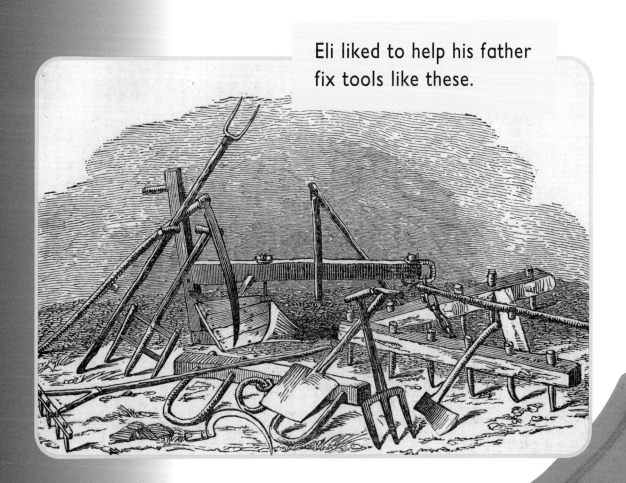

Trying New Things

Eli was interested in many things. When he was eight, he took apart his father's watch to see how it worked. Then, he put it back together as good as new.

Old watches had many small parts that were difficult to put together.

This person is making nails using a hammer and an anvil.

When he was older, Eli suggested that his father build a **forge** to make nails to sell. The business did well. Later, Eli used the forge to make hatpins and walking sticks.

Working and Studying

When Eli was 19 years old, he decided to go to college. He worked hard to earn money for school. Eli started Yale College when he was 23 years old.

Yale College is now called Yale University.

Eli finished college when he was 27. He wanted to become a **lawyer.** But he could not afford to go to school any longer. He had to find a job and earn money.

Eli would have to do a lot of studying to become a lawyer.

Going to Georgia

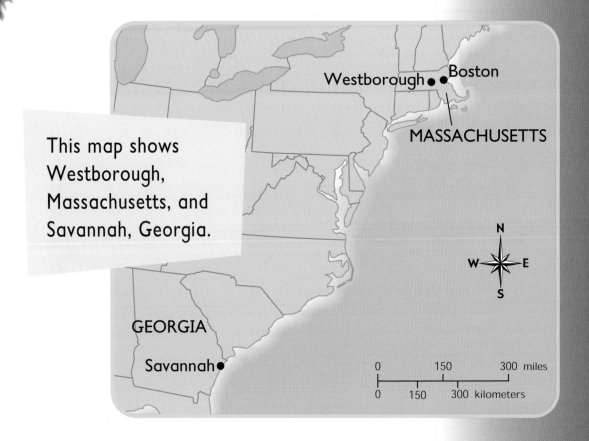

This map shows Westborough, Massachusetts, and Savannah, Georgia.

Eli got a job as a **tutor** in Savannah, Georgia. He traveled there by wagon and boat. But when Eli reached Georgia, he found out he did not have the job after all.

On the trip, Eli met Catherine Greene and Phineas Miller. Catherine owned Mulberry Grove, a **plantation** in Georgia. Phineas was the plantation **manager.** Catherine invited Eli to visit them.

This is a painting of Catherine Greene.

The First Cotton Gin

Seeds must be removed so the fluffy cotton can be used to make thread.

At Mulberry Grove Eli met other **plantation** owners. They talked about how hard it was to get seeds out of **cotton bolls.** They wanted a machine to do it.

Eli made a **model** of a machine called a **cotton gin.** Phineas Miller gave Eli money to improve the invention. In a few months, Eli made a machine that pulled seeds out of cotton faster than a person could.

Visitors can see the model of Eli's first cotton gin at the Smithsonian Museum in Washington, D.C.

Eli's Big Idea

This drawing shows how Eli's cotton gin works.

Eli got a **patent** on his invention so no one could copy his idea. Then, he went to New Haven, Connecticut. He bought land and started a shop where he could make **cotton gins.**

Visitors can see this cotton gin on display at the Eli Whitney Museum.

Eli did not want to make cotton gins one at a time. He had a new idea. He invented different machines to make each part of the gin. Then, the finished parts could be put together quickly.

Starting Over

In 1795 Eli's shop burned down with all the machines inside. Eli built the shop again. But his business did not do well. Although Eli had a **patent**, other people started making **cotton gins,** too.

This is a different kind of cotton gin made by Hogden Holmes.

Eli planned to sell his guns to the U.S. **Army.**

Eli was not earning much money. He decided to start a new business. He would make guns instead of cotton gins.

A New Way to Make Guns

Making each part of a gun by hand took a long time.

Eli had never made a gun before. Still, he was sure he could do it. He would make different machines to make the gun parts. That way, he could make guns more quickly than anyone else.

Eli wrote a letter to the U.S. **government.**
He said he could make all the guns the
army needed. In 1798 the government
hired Eli to make 10,000 guns in two years.

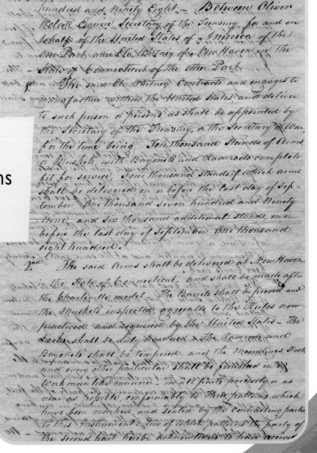

Eli signed this paper
agreeing to make guns
for the government.

A New Factory

Eli built an **armory** at Mill Rock, near New Haven. He made different machines that would make each part of a gun. Then he hired people to run the machines.

This drawing shows Eli's armory. An armory is a **factory** where guns are made.

Eli's armory made different types of guns.

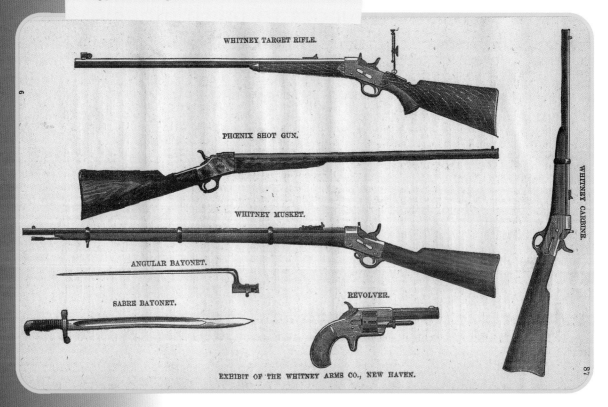

WHITNEY TARGET RIFLE.

PHŒNIX SHOT GUN.

WHITNEY MUSKET.

ANGULAR BAYONET.

SABRE BAYONET.

REVOLVER.

WHITNEY CARBINE.

EXHIBIT OF THE WHITNEY ARMS CO., NEW HAVEN.

It took Eli much longer to make the machines than he had thought. But the **government** liked the guns he made because they were of good quality.

Working Hard

It took about 10 years to finish making the 10,000 guns. Eli did not mind working for so long. He did not have a wife or children. Work was the most important thing in his life.

This is an old **advertisement** for Eli's **armory.**

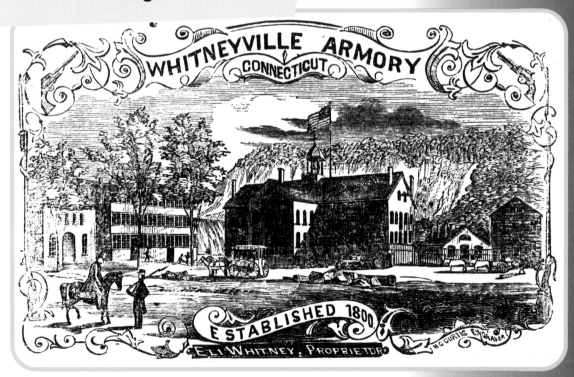

But Eli cared about other people, too. He built houses for his workers and their families. He also helped his sister by taking care of his three nephews.

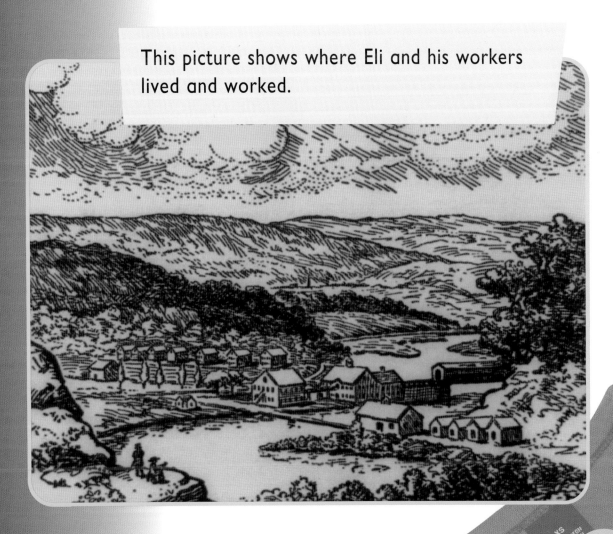

This picture shows where Eli and his workers lived and worked.

The Later Years

In 1817 Eli married Henrietta Edwards. They had four children. After Eli died in 1825, his nephews ran his business.

Eli's nephews continued to make quality guns.

This airplane factory uses mass production.

Eli's idea about how to make things is even more important than what he made. Today, his idea is called **mass production.** **Factories** around the world use it to make things quickly and cheaply.

Learning More About Eli Whitney

Some of Eli's ideas are still used to make **cotton gins.** But today's cotton gins are much bigger and faster than those that Eli made.

These are modern-day cotton gins.

This building is part of the Eli Whitney Museum.

There is an Eli Whitney Museum in Hamden, Connecticut. Visitors can see some of the buildings and machines that Eli built.

Fact File

- Eli's invention made cotton the most important crop in the South. Before the **cotton gin,** it took too long to clean cotton, so farmers did not earn much money by growing it.

- The cotton gin had actually been around for hundreds of years in countries like India. But these gins did not work on the kind of cotton grown in the United States. Eli's was the first that did.

- Eli built his **armory** near a waterfall so he could use water to power the machines that made the gun parts.

- The word *gin* in cotton gin is short for *engine*.

Timeline

1765	Eli Whitney is born in Westborough, Massachusetts, on December 8.
1789	Eli begins his studies at Yale College.
1792	Eli graduates from Yale.
	Eli heads to Savannah, Georgia.
	Eli spends time at Mulberry Grove **plantation.**
1793	Eli makes a **model** of his first cotton gin.
1794	Eli receives a **patent** on his invention.
1798	Eli agrees to make 10,000 guns for the U.S. **government.**
1817	Eli marries Henrietta Edwards.
1825	Eli Whitney dies on January 8.

Glossary

advertisement   something that tells people about a product to try to get them to buy it

armory   workshop or factory where guns or other weapons are made

army   people and equipment used to defend a country and keep it safe

cotton boll   fluffy white part of the cotton plant

cotton gin   machine that removes seeds from cotton bolls. Gin is short for engine.

factory   place where a product is made

forge   workshop with a furnace for heating metal so it can be shaped

government   group of people who rule a country

lawyer   person trained in the laws of a country

manager   person who is in charge of someone else's business or property

mass production   system where different machines make different parts. All the parts from one machine are the same. The parts are then put together to make a product.

model   small copy of a thing

patent   government papers that give an inventor the right to be the only one to make something

plantation   large farm that usually grows one main crop

tutor   teacher who works with one student or a small group of students

More Books to Read

Bagley, Katie. *Eli Whitney: American Inventor*. Mankato, Minn.: Capstone, 2003.

Cefrey, Holly. *The Inventions of Eli Whitney: The Cotton Gin*. New York: Rosen, 2003.

Gaines, Ann. *Eli Whitney*. Vero Beach, Fla.: Rourke, 2002.

Index